Nose cone

HOW SCIENCE WORKS
ROCKETS
AND OTHER SPACECRAFT

JOHN FARNDON

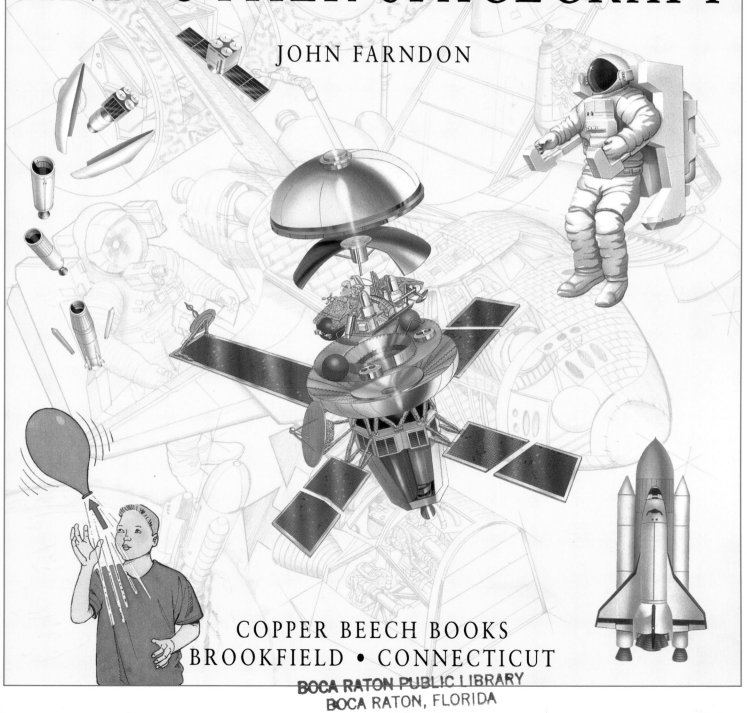

COPPER BEECH BOOKS
BROOKFIELD • CONNECTICUT

CONTENTS

INTRODUCTION

The rockets that launch spacecraft into
space are huge and powerful. Yet they
work in much the same way as fireworks.
Both get their power by burning fuel. As
they burn, hot gases push out of the back
of the rocket. This drives
the rocket forward.

This book tells you about all kinds of rockets and
spacecraft. It also reveals how the astronauts that fly
them cope with life in space. Some chapters come with
a project. If you do all of them, you can build a rocket
that soars high into the sky.

To make the projects, you will
need: a plastic bottle, paper,
cardboard, balsa wood, a craft
knife, a drill, scissors, craft glue,
strong epoxy glue, a ruler, a pencil,
oil-based paints, tinfoil, a cork,
and a bicycle pump and valve.

Rocket
project box

Science experiment
project box

© Aladdin Books Ltd 2000

Designed and produced by
Aladdin Books Ltd
28 Percy Street
London W1P 0LD

First published in
the United States in 2000 by
Copper Beech Books,
an imprint of
The Millbrook Press
2 Old New Milford Road
Brookfield, Connecticut 06804

ISBN 0-7613-1164-5 (Lib.bdg.)
ISBN 0-7613-0840-7 (Trade Pbk.)
Cataloging-in-Publication data is
on file at the Library of Congress
Printed in Belgium
All rights reserved

Editor
Jim Pipe

Science Consultant
Bryson Gore

Series Design
David West Children's Books

Designer
Simon Morse

Illustrators
Ian Thompson, Catherine Ward,
Don Simpson – Specs Art,
Simon Tegg, Graham White,
Alex Pang, Francis Phillipps,
Simon Bishop, and
Richard Rockwood

Picture Research
Brooks Krikler Research

THE SCIENCE OF SPACE

Huge teams of scientists are needed to develop the technology to send spacecraft into space. They have to build powerful rockets to lift the spacecraft above the earth against the pull of Earth's gravity.

Once in space, some spacecraft are controlled by automation from the ground. Others have a crew, and the spacecraft must be built to carry them safely.

Rocket fuels burn so fiercely that rockets must be built from special materials. See more on page 14.

CONTROLS

There are no wheels to steer with in space. Instead, spacecraft are guided by small "booster" rockets on the side. These are turned to push the spacecraft in the right direction.

Nose cone

Satellite

Outer shell

Mir space station

Space shuttle

LIVING IN SPACE

Once in space, the crew are out on their own. The spacecraft must provide all their needs and protect them from dangerous radiation. In space, the spacecraft is free of the pull of gravity, which holds things down on the ground. This makes even showering tricky!

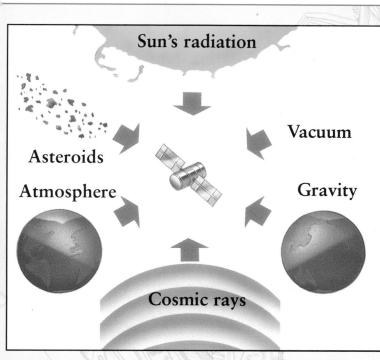

Sun's radiation

Asteroids

Atmosphere

Vacuum

Gravity

Cosmic rays

WHAT IS SPACE?

Rocket scientists have to think about what space is like. Gravity and Earth's atmosphere still affect a spacecraft when it is in orbit, but the vacuum that exists in space creates other problems, too.

Harmful rays from the sun and the rest of the universe can also damage a spacecraft, as can even tiny pieces of floating rock.

Venera

CONSTRUCTION

Lunar module

Most rockets are quite similar, but the small spacecraft they carry vary enormously. Venera was made to visit Venus. The lunar probe was designed for an unmanned visit to the moon. The lunar module was designed to land astronauts on the moon's surface. Learn more about spacecraft on page 22.

Fuel tanks

Lunar probe

The spacecraft takes off as soon as the main rocket engines are fired. This is a dangerous time, and during the final countdown to "liftoff" the area around the rocket is completely cleared. Turn to page 10 to learn about rocket power.

Burner where the fuels burn

CHAPTER 1 – INTO SPACE

One of the hardest things for spacecraft to do is to actually get off the ground. To climb into space, a spacecraft needs to overcome gravity, the force of attraction that holds everything on the ground. So far, the only way scientists have found of doing this is to use huge rockets to thrust spacecraft upward against gravity.

Break out! If a rocket is launched with enough power, it can break free of Earth's gravity.

When you hold a tennis ball and a grapefruit (*above*), the different weights that you feel are the force of Earth's gravity pulling on their two different masses.

Mass and weight

Fill a balloon with water and it feels very heavy. Now lower the balloon into water. You will see that it feels much lighter. This is because the pressure of the water outside is lifting it up. Weight is a measure of the pull of gravity, and it can change. This is why scientists talk about "mass." This is the amount of matter in an object. It's the same wherever you measure it.

Airplanes only climb a short way above the earth, where the pull of gravity is still strong.

GRAVITY

Gravity doesn't only hold things on the ground. It is the force of attraction between every bit of matter in the universe. It is the force that makes the earth and all the other planets stay close to the sun and continue circling it.

Sun

Moon

The moon stays in orbit (circling the earth) because the moon and Earth are pulled together by each other's gravity.

Satellites stay up because they are moving too fast to fall. Their speed balances out the pull of Earth's gravity.

Gravity gets weaker higher up, so a satellite circling the earth low down has to travel much faster to stay up.

LOSING WEIGHT

Astronauts in spacecraft orbiting the earth float around freely as if they were weightless. This is because the spacecraft is whizzing around the earth so fast that a force, called centrifugal force, balances the effect of gravity. Astronauts practice being weightless by flying in a plane that falls so fast that they float off the floor (*top*).

FORCES NEEDED

Airplanes use the pressure of air on their wings to lift them up. But there is no air far above the earth and wings would be useless.

So rocket engines alone must develop enough "thrust," or push, to overcome the spacecraft's weight.

The British scientist Sir Isaac Newton (1642–1727) discovered many of the laws about momentum. Momentum is what keeps a moving object going in a straight line unless a force acts on it.

TYPES OF ENERGY

Energy comes in two forms. Potential energy (PE) is energy stored up ready for action, like the unburned fuel in a rocket.

Kinetic energy (KE) is the energy something has because it is moving, like a rocket traveling through space.

NEWTON'S FIRST LAW

Newton's first law states that to make an object go faster or slower, you need a force. This is because its momentum keeps it going at the same speed and in the same direction. If an astronaut pushed himself away from a spacecraft, he could drift off into space forever, as there is nothing in space to stop him.

A spacecraft coming back to Earth is traveling very fast, but it relies on friction with the air to slow it down. This is why it gets very hot.

TRAVEL IN SPACE

Moving through space is very different from moving on the ground. When a car moves, its wheels push against the ground. As soon as they stop pushing, friction slows the car down. In empty space, there is nothing to stop a spacecraft from moving – but there is nothing to push against either, not even air. So how does a spacecraft move?

Skylab

Space stations need only a little power to keep them in orbit because they are moving through space very fast, so they have a lot of momentum.

In space, a rocket is kept going by its own momentum and a few bursts from booster rockets.

The secret of space travel

You can't push unless there's something to push against. Newton's third law shows how, when a force pushes one way, an equal force pushes in the opposite direction. If you throw a ball while on roller skates, you will roll back a little in reaction as the ball moves forward. Rockets move through space in the same way.

As the burning fuels expand behind a rocket, they push it forward in an equal and opposite reaction. When an astronaut opens a hatch in space, her body also turns in an opposite reaction.

NEWTON'S SECOND LAW

The amount something speeds up or slows down – the acceleration – depends on just how strong the force is and how heavy the object is. The heavier a rocket is, the more force it needs to get it into space. A big car is also harder to get moving than a small car.

Some rockets, such as booster rockets, burn a solid, rubbery fuel, but most are powered by liquid fuel. Liquid fuel only burns with oxygen, but there is no oxygen far above the ground. So the rocket must also carry a chemical that provides oxygen, called an oxidizer. The fuel and oxidizer mix in a combustion chamber, then a spark called an igniter sets them alight.

Blow up a balloon and let it go. It darts about as it reacts against the air rushing out of it. Rockets work in much the same way.

Ariane V blasts off

Fuel tank

Oxidizer tank

Turbine

Pump   Pump

Injectors

Valve   Valve

Combustion chamber

Nozzle

Too narrow   Too wide

LIQUID FUEL ROCKETS

Different rockets use different fuels – the space shuttle uses liquid hydrogen, and Saturn V used kerosene. Most types of fuel are pumped into the combustion chamber with an oxidizer such as liquid oxygen (or LOX). Here, they burn together to create a high pressure stream of gases that roars out through a small nozzle at speeds of about 9,000 mph.

The nozzle is shaped so that the gases roar out of the rocket at the maximum speed and pressure.

For the first few minutes of flight, the rocket's speed is limited by gravity and, as it speeds up, friction with the air. As it climbs higher, these get less and less.

As it burns more fuel, the rocket itself gets lighter. Once in space, it needs only a little fuel to keep it going.

Fuel line

Liquid oxygen

Liquid hydrogen

LIQUID FUEL ROCKET

Nozzle

MODEL ROCKET
PART 1
NOZZLE

1 Find a cork that fits a half gallon plastic bottle. Then ask an adult to drill a hole through it just wide enough for a valve to fit tightly.

2 Seal the surface of the cork by painting craft glue over the outside of it, but leave the hole free of glue.

3 When the glue is dry, push the valve through the hole in the cork. Use the same sort of valve you would use to pump up a football or basketball.

ARIANE V

Rocket fuel burns incredibly quickly, and most rockets only have enough fuel to last a few minutes. The main engine in the Ariane V rocket (see page 10) burns for ten minutes. In this time it uses 158 tons of fuel.

Ariane V

MMUs

MMU

You don't have to burn rocket fuel to move around in space. Forcing any gas out through a nozzle will provide a push in the opposite direction.

The Manned Maneuvering Units (MMUs) that astronauts strap on their backs for spacewalks use jets of cold nitrogen gas in this way.

Nozzles pointing in different directions (*right*) move the MMU and steer it in the direction the astronaut wants to go.

OTHER ROCKET ENGINES

In rockets powered with liquid fuels, the fuels weigh an enormous amount and are dangerously explosive. So space engineers have experimented with other engines.

Solid-fuel rockets are already used. But scientists are trying other ideas, including NERVA engines (*below*). These pump hydrogen gas at high pressure into a nuclear reactor. This creates a powerful jet that propels the rocket into space.

Booster

NERVA ENGINE

Bottles pump in hydrogen

Liquid oxygen

Liquid hydrogen

Solid fuel

Once ignited, solid-fuel engines usually cannot be stopped or restarted, so they are generally used for short missions or for small booster rockets that make fine changes to direction.

SOLID-FUEL ROCKETS

Parachutes allow boosters to fall back to Earth

Solid-fuel rocket engines are the oldest of all engines. They were used by the Chinese almost a thousand years ago. They are basically rods of solid fuel with a tube down the middle. When the fuel is ignited, it burns out through the tube. In the space shuttle, the fuel lasts about two minutes.

Nuclear reactor

Nozzle

A-1 Sputnik   Titan 34D   CZ-4   Energia

THE NEW SHUTTLE

If the Venture Star (*below*) is a success, flights into space could be as routine as flights on an airplane. With its "linear airspike" engines – rockets arranged in rows – Venture Star can take off and land again and again like an airplane.

ACE HUTTLE

Cargo bay

Main engine

Wings for gliding

Rocket launchers have grown bigger and bigger over the last 50 years (*above*).

The space shuttle is one of the few spacecraft that uses solid-fuel rockets to boost it into space. The shuttle has two solid-rocket boosters (SRBs) as well as three main engines, each powered by liquid fuel from a big strap-on tank.

DANGER: EXPLOSIVE!

Scientists do all they can to reduce accidents, but space travel is risky. When a spacecraft takes off on liquid-fuel rockets, it is riding on a giant bomb. In 1986, the space shuttle Challenger (*below*) blew up on liftoff.

Third stage

Nose cone falls away

Satellite

Most satellites need to be protected to cope with the force of gravity during liftoff. Some are launched inside the nose cone of the rocket, which falls away just like the booster sections (*left*).

Second stage

Boosters

CONSTRUCTION

To cope with the kind of energy needed to thrust a spacecraft high into the sky, rockets have to be incredibly tough. Temperatures in the combustion chamber of a solid-fuel rocket can soar well over 5000° F. Yet rockets have to be light, too. So engineers build them from tough, light materials such as titanium.

First stage

MODEL ROCKET
PART 2
THE BODY & FINS

1 Use the plan at the end of the book to mark out a fin onto balsa wood. Then get an adult to help you cut out four identical fins using a craft knife.

2 Glue the fins to the bottom of a half gallon plastic bottle with strong epoxy glue, so that they form a cross pattern (*right*).

BOOSTER STAGES

The amount of fuel needed to launch most spacecraft is still so huge that most rockets are simply giant fuel tanks. Once a spacecraft has escaped the pull of Earth's gravity, there is no need for all this fuel. So the rockets are built in stages that fall away as the spacecraft climbs higher and fuel is burned up.

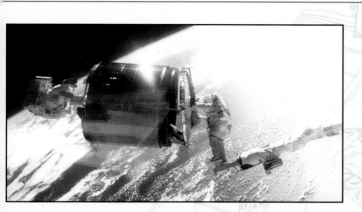

LIGHT BUT STRONG

Rockets are built like giant tin cans. It's easy to squeeze a soda can in at the sides. But you'll find it's almost impossible to squeeze it from the ends. This is because the rigid rim of the can spreads the pressure of your squeeze through the length of the can. Rockets are light and strong in the same way.

Space stations that are far too big to launch are put together in space, bit by bit, by astronauts (*above*).

The sides of some rockets are not thick metal sheets, but two thin sheets separated by a honeycomb of very thin metal boxes (*right*). This structure is light and strong.

First stage

Second stage

Third stage

SATURN V ROCKET

Lunar modules

Lunar modules

Third stage

Second stage

First stage

SHAPES IN SPACE

On Earth, friction between the air and a vehicle's surface causes drag. This force slows a vehicle down. Out in space, there is no air, and it doesn't really matter what shape a spacecraft is. Probes (*right*) are often awkward shapes, with parts sticking out at all angles.

Spacecraft coming back to Earth have a flat front, so that the air acts as a brake.

Rockets have a pointed nose to slice through the air.

The Viking probe (*below*) was sent to look for life on Mars.

DRAG

Drag is a force that slows moving objects down when a gas or liquid flows past them. You can feel the effect of drag by pulling your hand through a bowl of water.

Viking lander

Solar panels

Fuel tanks

Solar panels catch the sun's rays and provide probes with energy.

MODEL ROCKET
PART 3
THE NOSE

3 Then glue the nose cone to the base of the plastic bottle – the top of the rocket.

1 Cut out the nose cone shape from cardboard using the plan at the end of this book.

2 To make the cone, overlap the two straight sides of the nose cone shape and glue them together.

THE PAYLOAD

When a spacecraft takes off, most of its weight is fuel and fuel tanks. The space shuttle weighs only 75 tons, but the total weight of the fuel tanks, rockets, and fuel needed to blast it into space is 2,000 tons. The amount the shuttle can carry in its cargo bay is just 30 tons.

The payload is what rockets carry into space, such as (*above*):
a) probe – a spacecraft with no crew
b) mission with human crew
c) satellites

REENTRY

When the wind blows very hard, it can make your face sting. But imagine the force when a shuttle traveling at over 12,000 mph reenters the earth's atmosphere. The friction with the air makes the shuttle very hot. So its nose and underside are coated with heat-resistant ceramic tiles.

During their descent, spacecraft are pulled by gravity like any other object. In the past, small space capsules used parachutes to slow the last bit of their fall (*right*).

Shuttles fly back to Earth under their own power – like an airplane.

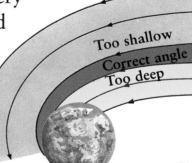

A shuttle must reenter at the correct angle. If it comes in too shallow, it bounces off the atmosphere; if it aims too deep, it burns up.

CHAPTER 3 – WHAT IS SPACE?

As you go higher and higher, the earth's atmosphere gets thinner and thinner. Eventually, about 550 miles up, it fades away into space.

Space is the vast, black emptiness between planets and stars. In space, there is not even air to breathe. But it is constantly crossed by streams of dangerous radiation from the sun and other stars.

WHERE IT STARTS

It is hard to say where the atmosphere ends and space begins. For astronauts, space starts at 80 miles above the earth, the lowest height a spacecraft can stay in orbit. On the ground you can drive that distance in an hour – so space is not far from the surface of our planet.

The atmosphere only fades off into empty space in a layer called the exosphere. The exosphere is about 480 miles above ground.

Gasp!

A portion of air is oxygen, the gas most things, such as rocket fuel, need to burn. But there is no oxygen (or any other gas) in space. To see what happens when oxygen is used up, get an adult to try this experiment.

1 Stand a candle in a shallow bowl of water. The water makes sure no extra air can reach the candle.
2 Light the candle. Place a glass jar over it. After a while, the candle goes out. This is because most of the oxygen in the jar has been used up.

Thermosphere (50-480 miles up)
Temp. from -248°F to 3632°F.

Jet

Surface

Sea level – The temperature on the surface is about 52°F.

MODEL ROCKET
PART 3

PROTECTION

1 Use acrylic paint to paint the rocket's nose and tail fins. Wrap tinfoil around the body of the rocket, with the shiny side facing outward.

2 Try this experiment to see how spacecraft can be protected in space. Fill two bottles with water. Wrap one in tinfoil and paint the other black. Leave them in the sunshine. After an hour, feel each bottle. The bottle wrapped in foil will feel much cooler than the black one, because the sun's rays bounce off the shiny foil.

Spacesuits stop astronauts from getting too hot or cold. They also shield against the sun's rays. We are normally protected from these rays by the earth's atmosphere (but we can get sunburned).

Shuttle

Stratosphere (8-34 miles up) Temp. from -106° to 50°F.

EARTH

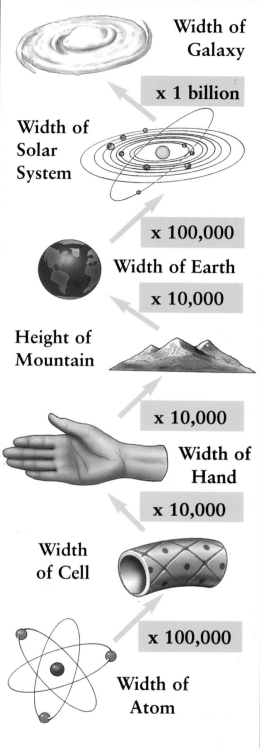

Width of Galaxy

x 1 billion

Width of Solar System

x 100,000

Width of Earth

x 10,000

Height of Mountain

x 10,000

Width of Hand

x 10,000

Width of Cell

x 100,000

Width of Atom

Astronomers only began to realize how big space is about 70 years ago. The chart above shows you just how big space is, compared to things around us.

SATELLITES

Artificial satellites are the 2,000 or so spacecraft that circle the earth nonstop. They circle at a height where their speed perfectly matches the pull of Earth's gravity.

They whizz around the earth just too fast to be pulled down by gravity – yet not so fast that they fly off into space.

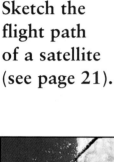

Sketch the flight path of a satellite (see page 21).

The Hubble Space Telescope (or HST, *below*) has taken the only accurate pictures of the tiny and distant planet Pluto and has revealed the best evidence for black holes in space.

Radio antenna

SATELLITES

There are many kinds of satellites. Communications satellites, for instance, bounce telephone and radio signals around the world.

Weather satellites show the weather from above. In the picture on the left, a satellite is being repaired by astronauts on a space shuttle.

Mirror B

Cylinder

Mirror A

Instruments and cameras

HUBBLE SPACE TELESCOPE

Telescopes in orbit get a clear view of objects in space because there is no atmosphere to affect their view. The most famous is the Hubble Space Telescope. It gathers light in the cylinder, which is reflected by mirror A toward mirror B. This then reflects the image back toward cameras and other scientific instruments

SATELLITE PATHS

Satellites circle the earth at different heights above the ground. The highest ones orbit at exactly the same speed that the earth is turning, so they seem to stay in the same place above the earth. Satellites lower down seem to pass over the surface of the earth in a wavy path (*right*).

First pass

Second pass – path changes as the earth spins

Solar panels

The HST could spot a coin 400 miles away!

Instruments and cameras

It can be tricky to repair a satellite when it is traveling so fast. A shuttle crew must choose exactly the right speed to match the satellite's orbit.

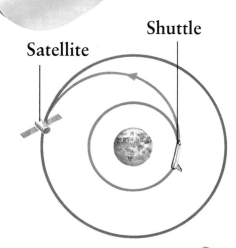

Satellite

Shuttle

Satellite orbit

Try this experiment to see why satellite paths seem wavy.

1 Cut a piece of paper and tape it around a tin can. Then draw a line down the middle of the paper. The line is the "equator."

2 Draw a straight line around the can at an angle to the first line, as shown. This is the satellite's orbit.

3 Unwrap the paper and see how the straight line has become wavy!

To see how satellites turn in space, hold onto a bicycle wheel by the hub and sit on a swivel chair. Get an adult to spin the wheel very rapidly. Try tilting the wheel and you will find that the effect is to swivel you one way or the other on the chair.

Thrusters

MOVING IN SPACE

Out in space, spacecraft don't have to deal with the powerful pull of Earth's gravity or push their way through the atmosphere. There are, however, still plenty of problems with moving in space – especially for probes that need to turn just a little bit for the right camera angle.

Many spacecraft have a set of thruster rockets. These are small rockets with nozzles pointing in different directions. To change direction, the spacecraft fires particular sets of nozzles.

Probe spins the other way.

Reaction wheel spins one way.

Giotto

Probes such as Giotto and Galileo have gyroscopic systems to control the way they are pointing. These use a heavy spinning wheel called a reaction wheel, like the bicycle wheel on the swivel chair (*top*). When a small motor changes the angle of the reaction wheel, the momentum of the spinning reaction wheel makes the whole probe swivel.

Galileo

SLINGSHOT EFFECT

Many space probes traveling through the solar system use the planets to help them on their way. They fly close enough to a planet to use the pull of its gravity to accelerate them on through space, on a different course. It is a bit like a stone being spun around and hurled from an old-fashioned sling, which is why this is called the slingshot effect.

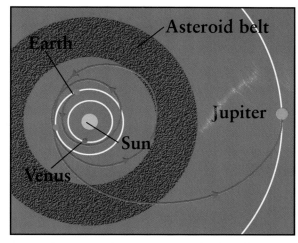

Galileo used Venus and Earth in a "slingshot" toward Jupiter (*above*).

MOON LANDING

When the Apollo space missions landed men on the moon, the main "command module" continued circling the moon in space. The astronauts touched down on the moon's surface in a small, light "lunar module" little bigger than a trailer. This had its own rockets to let it down slowly and boost it back into space.

Lunar module

Unlike the moon, Mars has a thick atmosphere. So when the *Mars Sojourner* landed there in 1997, it could use a parachute to slow its fall. It also inflated its own airbags to soften the landing.

CHAPTER 4 – LIVING IN SPACE

When astronauts travel into space, the spacecraft must not only protect them from radiation of space, but it must also provide all they need in order to breathe, eat, drink, and sleep. Once in orbit, the astronauts have to deal with weightlessness. This means that things float freely because gravity does not hold them down.

To run, the equipment onboard a spacecraft needs a lot of energy. In addition to solar panels (*above*), spacecraft have batteries to store electricity for use when they are in the earth's shadow.

Port to link up with other spacecraft

Escape capsule

Laboratories

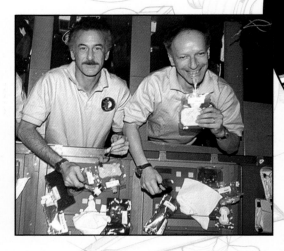

SPACE FOOD

Space food must be healthy and easy to use and store. On early missions, astronauts ate dried and powdered food to which they added water. Now they have prepared meals, like microwave meals at home (*above*).

When the International Space Station (*below*) is finished, it will be 355 ft long and 295 ft wide.

It will provide a complete environment for dozens of people to work in space for months at a time.

KEEPING A BALANCE

To survive, astronauts need oxygen as well as food and drink (*below*). Machines in spacecraft provide oxygen and remove the carbon dioxide that the astronauts breathe out. Space toilets (*left*) save the water from bodily waste and blast the dry matter into space.

THE HUMAN SYSTEM

Food

Water

Oxygen

IN

Solar panels

Living quarters

OUT

Sweat

Carbon dioxide

Bodily waste

BIODOMES

Only Earth allows humans to live without any protection. If we are ever to live on other planets, it will have to be inside completely sealed buildings (like the Biosphere 2 experiment, *left*) that provide all our needs, just like a spacecraft.

COMMUNICATIONS

Even far out in space, astronauts and spacecraft can keep in touch with mission control on the ground in a number of ways.

The launch

Astronauts talk to mission control by radio. Television pictures are beamed back to Earth. Computers, sensors, and other equipment on the spacecraft send back streams of signals via radio waves.

This shuttle cockpit (*above*) shows the huge number of control systems that are needed in a spacecraft.

Sometimes signals can be beamed directly between the space shuttle and mission control.

Shuttle

Relay satellite

When the shuttle is out of sight, signals sometimes have to be bounced off a relay satellite.

MISSION CONTROL

Mission control (*above*) follows every spacecraft constantly, but the link is not always easy to maintain. Sometimes the spacecraft may move out of sight on the other side of the world, or on the far side of a planet. Important messages are often printed out so they can be checked.

Fuel tanks released

Launch satellite

Maneuver for reentry

Release boosters

Reentry

MODEL ROCKET
PART 5
BLAST OFF!

1 Pour about two cups of water into your rocket and place the cork firmly into the neck of the bottle. Attach a bicycle pump to the valve in the cork and stand the rocket on its fins on a hard surface outside. Pump air into your rocket until it blasts off.

WARNING: DO NOT STAND OVER THE ROCKET AS THE AIR IS PUMPED IN.

2 Find out what level of water gives the best results.

Glides back to Earth

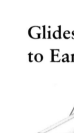

Blast off

SHUTTLE MISSION

The space shuttle was the first reusable spacecraft. It is often used for carrying satellites into space or repairing them in orbit. It is also used to ferry crew members to and from space stations.

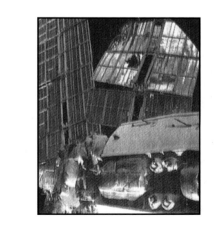

If your car breaks down, you can take it to be repaired. In space, it's not quite so easy! When the Mir space station got damaged (*left*), it cost millions of dollars to keep it in orbit. In the end, the station was abandoned.

SCIENCE PRINCIPLES

LOOK BACK AND TEST YOUR KNOWLEDGE

NEWTON'S FIRST LAW

Newton's First Law of Motion is about changes in movement. It states that whenever something moves, even the least bit differently, there is a force involved. When something starts to move, speeds up, slows down, or simply changes direction, there is a force involved. It has to do with inertia and momentum.

MOMENTUM

Everything that is standing still has inertia. This means it won't move unless something forces it to. Everything that is moving has momentum. This means it won't slow down or speed up unless something forces it to. Something heavy and fast, like a car, has a lot of momentum. It's the car's momentum that crushes it if it crashes into a wall (*above*).

 (1) Why does a shuttle have wings? Answers to all questions on pages 28-29 are on page 32.

NEWTON'S SECOND LAW

Newton's Second Law of Motion is about how effective a force is. The amount something speeds up or slows down is the acceleration. Newton's Second Law states that acceleration depends on how big the force is and how heavy the object is. To throw a heavy ball fast, you need a strong throw.

 (2) What do you think falls faster, a bullet or a marble dropped from the same height?

NEWTON'S THIRD LAW

When you walk, the ground pushes up against your feet with the same force. If it didn't, your feet would sink into the ground just like they do into water. If the ground pushed harder, it would fire you into the air.

Whenever anything moves, there is always this balance of forces working in opposite reactions.

GRAVITY

Gravity is the natural force that pulls everything together. Every bit of matter in the universe has its own gravitational pull. The strength of the pull depends how far apart things are and how big they are – or rather, their mass, which is how much matter they are made of.

Big, heavy objects pull harder than small, light objects. This is why Earth's gravity is strong enough to hold us on the ground, yet we can't even feel an egg's gravity.

? *(3) Would a full bag feel lighter or heavier as you get farther away from the earth?* (clue above)

RADIATION

Radiation is a spreading of energy. Sometimes you can see it. The light you see things by is a kind of radiation. The world is warm and bright because the sun radiates light and heat (*below*). Most radiation, though, is invisible, like X rays and radio waves.

TECHNICAL TERMS

Booster – An additional rocket designed to propel a spacecraft farther on its journey.

Centrifugal force – A force that seems to throw you outward when you move in a circle. When a satellite is in orbit, this force is exactly balanced by gravity.

Liquid fuel – Rocket fuel carried in liquid form, such as kerosene.

Manned Maneuvering Unit – The rocket-powered backpack that moves an astronaut around on spacewalks.

Orbit – A complete circuit around something – often by a satellite or spacecraft held close to a planet by gravity.

Oxidizer – The source of oxygen needed for liquid fuel to burn.

Payload – The items that are carried on spacecraft, such as astronauts and equipment.

Reentry – The point at which a spacecraft returning to Earth enters Earth's atmosphere from space. As it reenters, friction with the air in Earth's atmosphere makes the spacecraft very hot.

Satellite – Anything that circles another object in space. Moons are natural satellites. Artificial satellites are spacecraft that circle the earth.

Thrust – The "strength" of a rocket engine – that is, how powerfully it pushes.

SPACECRAFT PARTS

There are two main kinds of spacecraft currently in use. First, there is the planelike space shuttle that carries astronauts into low space orbits. Then there are unmanned spacecraft that carry probes and satellites into space tucked inside a nose cone.

SPACE SHUTTLE

Two solid-fuel rocket boosters power the shuttle into the air for two minutes after the launch.

1 MAIN ENGINES

These continue after the boosters fall away. They are fueled by a big external tank.

2 VERTICAL STABILIZER

Like an airplane's tail, the vertical stabilizer helps the shuttle steer.

3 WINGS

The shuttle uses wings to glide through the air after it reenters the atmosphere.

4 FLIGHT DECK

Two of the crew sit on the flight deck during launch and reentry. Here they can control the shuttle.

5 CARGO BAY

The shuttle has a big cargo bay for carrying things such as satellites into space. This can be opened without affecting the crew compartments.

WHERE ARE THEY?

Can you guess where pictures A–C were taken? One is on Mars, one is on the moon, and one is near the earth. Which one is which?

SATURN V

6 FIRST STAGE
The first stage of a rocket is always the biggest, providing the huge thrust needed to push the spacecraft vertically off the ground.

7 SECOND STAGE
Once the first stage has launched the rocket, it burns out and drops away. Then the second stage fires to push the rocket faster and farther up.

8 THIRD STAGE
The third stage gives the rocket its final push to a speed where it is free of Earth's gravity.

PAYLOAD
A-C are different kinds of payload carried inside the nose cone of spacecraft. One is for landing astronauts on the moon, one is a satellite, and one is a space probe. Can you guess which is which?

11 NOSE CONE
Inside the nose are the three spacecraft (below) used for a moon landing.

12 LUNAR MODULE
This takes astronauts down to the moon's surface.

9 OXIDIZER TANK
One tank provides the oxygen the fuel needs to burn (as there is no oxygen in space).

10 FUEL TANK
Another tank provides the fuel that can be burned when it is combined with oxygen.

13 SERVICE MODULE
This circles above the moon.

14 COMMAND MODULE
This carries the astronauts back to Earth.

INDEX

The finished model rocket

Answers to pages 28–29
1 A shuttle has wings so that it can glide down once it has reentered Earth's atmosphere.
2 Even though the bullet is traveling faster in a horizontal direction, the marble and the bullet fall at about the same speed. Because they weigh about the same, gravity pulls them down with the same force. 3 The bag would feel lighter the farther away from the earth you get, as the force of gravity gets less.

Answers to page 30
The moon = A, Mars = B, Earth = C.

Answers to page 31
Space probe = A, Satellite = B, Craft for landing on moon = C.

PHOTO CREDITS

Abbreviations – t–top, m–middle, b–bottom, r–right, l–left, c–center:

Cover and page 13m – Lockheed Martin. 4t, 13b, 17, 24m & 25b – Frank Spooner Pictures.

Page 6, 7 both, 10, 12, 13t, 15, 19, 20, 24b, 25t, 26 all, 27 & 30 all – National Aeronautics and Space Administration (NASA).